God's Sovereign Word Brings Victory

Books by Joan Hart

How to Have Victory through Prayer

Phenomena of the Holy Spirit

Faith and the Supernatural

Healing and the Miraculous

Divine Steps to Ministry

God's Sovereign Word Brings Victory

Joan Hart

iUniverse®

GOD'S SOVEREIGN WORD BRINGS VICTORY

iUniverse books may be ordered through booksellers or by contacting:

iUniverse
1663 Liberty Drive
Bloomington, IN 47403
www.iuniverse.com
1-800-Authors (1-800-288-4677)

ISBN: 978-1-5320-3107-6 (sc)
ISBN: 978-1-5320-3108-3 (e)

Print information available on the last page.

iUniverse rev. date: 05/20/2020

Preface

This book does not contain all the sovereign experiences I have received as a result of praying the Word. However I have chosen the ones that will benefit your faith and put the desire within you to pray the written Word.

DEDICATION

This book is dedicated to the Glory of God. Through His inspiration and the leading of the Holy Spirit, Scriptures were revealed to me to pray, so I might have victory in my life. This victory helps me reach out to others, helping them have victory in their lives through prayer.

TABLE OF CONTENTS

INTRODUCTION

After receiving Jesus Christ as my personal Savior, I began to read the Word. While reading, I discovered there were verses that are promises to me from the Lord. I began to highlight them and eventually wrote them down and then began to pray them. As I did this each day, answers to my prayers began to manifest. It wasn't long before other people wanted to have a copy of the verses I prayed so they too would have victory through their prayers. Throughout the years, many received my Scripture pages and learned how to pray the verses. Many testimonies have been received from those who had answers and victory through their prayers also.

The Lord revealed to my heart that this book is a tool that His children need, so they will have help getting through their hard days and years ahead. The Scriptures are for protection against the enemy. They will give strength to each one who prays them with faith and believing. They will be a tool to help each one learn how to pray the promises God has so freely given us.

My prayer is that all who read this book, and begin to speak the Scriptures out loud, will be blessed in their spiritual walk as they reach a new level of prayer and intimacy with the Lord, as well as, have a new hunger for His Word.

Everyone Has a Beginning

One cold, dark, winter night in 1975, my children, then six and two years old, were tucked into their warm beds, fast asleep. My husband, a salesman, was on the road traveling to get home for the weekend.

Usually, Dean called to let me know where he was and how long it would be until he arrived home. There were no such things as cell phones back then. So he would have to get off the highway, and find a phone to be able to call me. Late at night not many places were open for him to use a phone.

On this particular night, I hadn't heard from him. I should have been worried about him out on the icy roads, but instead I was filled with self-pity. I was consumed by the notion that he didn't care enough about me to let me know what time he was coming home! I felt a tremendous sense of despair and loneliness.

It was not unusual for me to be left alone while Dean was out working hard to support our family. But on this particular night, the devil took advantage of my weakened state of mind and began to tell me, as he had many other times, that my husband didn't love me, and that I was not needed. Unfortunately, I began to believe him, and because I believed his lies, I began entertaining thoughts of suicide. I did not know then, as I do now, how the enemy relentlessly attacks you and whips at your mind until you finally act on his evil suggestions.

It was getting very late, but I sat there in the dining room chair, staring out at the white sparkling snow, watching for my husband's car to come down the road. Everything was very still and quiet. Normally, a picture-perfect winter night like this would bring feelings of peace and tranquility. After all, I was safe in my warm home with our children. But instead, a shiver ran through me as I began to think about how alone I was. As I brooded, I began to plan my family's future life without me. I even chose another wife for my husband and a mother for our children. I couldn't take it anymore! It was two in the morning with still *no word* from my husband!

I rose from my chair in the dining room and headed for the living room. I had to go through the living room down the long hall to the bathroom where I would find a razor blade to slit my wrist. I figured it wouldn't be long before Dean would be home, and our children would be safe until then.

God is with Me

As I stepped into the large living room, I stopped and looked around. I felt so alone. I glanced down the long hallway toward the bathroom a moment and whispered to myself, "Oh, I am so alone!" As soon as I said those words, I heard an audible voice come from behind me. The voice said, "Lo, I am with you always." I recognized those words! I had learned them in Sunday school as a child! They were words that were written in the Bible!

I was raised by my parents in a traditional, denominational church. It seemed like my family went to church every time the doors were open. Our lives centered on all the usual activities. I loved to get together with the families and their children who were my age and whom I was growing up with. I enjoyed going to Sunday school, Vacation Bible School, youth group meetings, singing in the youth choir, and of course, enjoying the fellowship gatherings for those wonderful potluck suppers. Everyone was usually happy, and there was lots of laughter, as well as a time for instruction about the Lord.

This time of fun and training had made it possible for me to recognize the voice and the words I had just heard, were the Words of Jesus! Instantly, I felt the Presence of God and fell to my knees by the nearest chair in the living room. I told Jesus I was sorry for ever thinking of committing suicide. I said that if there was any truth, to what I had heard at a church youth retreat, about inviting Jesus into my heart so I would feel better, I wanted it to happen right now! I cried and cried as I told Him every wrong thing I had ever done. I had no way of knowing that the Holy Spirit was leading me to repent and He was saving my soul!

I got up off of my knees and stood there a moment trying to compose myself. I had never experienced anything like this before. I had such peace as I walked down the long hallway towards the bathroom, but instead turned and went into the bedroom, a changed person! I had the most peaceful rest I'd had in years.

A New Creation

My husband arrived home a short time later. He knew something had happened, because usually, if I didn't wait up for him, I went to bed with all the lights on due to having such fear. But on this particular night, I had turned off every light in the house. The fear was gone!

I did not share my experience with Dean for a long time, because I was not sure what had happened to me, but I did feel better. That much I knew for sure.

Taught by the Holy Spirit

During the first year after I received Jesus, I continued to attend the same denominational church. But I was no longer happy there. Something was missing; it was the Holy Spirit! But as of yet, I didn't understand what it meant to be filled with the Holy Spirit. I had never read the Bible before, but now I seemed to want to read it. Imagine that!

There were times I would be sitting in front of the television, minding my own business, when my eyes would travel to the Bible that was on the table. We always kept a

Bible in the living room---after all, every home has a Bible, right? Once I realized God wanted me to read it I said, "Oh, You want me to read it!"

I picked it up to read and tried to understand it, but it was a King James Version which made it very difficult. It seemed to be way over my head with all the *theses* and *thous* in it. By the time I figured out what was being said, it seemed like too much work to go on, so I would quit reading. I was frustrated to say the least. I shared this with my husband and he told me about a modern version of the Bible he had in his bathroom. He had picked it up for free in his travels and said if I wanted it, I could have it.

I quickly retrieved the Bible and began to read. Finally, I understood what I was reading, but I was still hungry for more knowledge. Eventually, I purchased a New International Version of the Bible which had even more clarity for me. I poured God's Word into me for about one year. Then I wanted to find someone else who felt the same way about the Bible, and the Lord, as I did. I wanted to share God's Word with them.

I had been a person who attended church all my life and had always believed I was a Christian, but now I realized I was not a Christian, only a person who attended church. Once I received Jesus Christ into my heart, then I did become a Christian, a born-again believer!

Maybe you have always attended church too, but have

never heard you need Jesus in your heart to go to Heaven. If you want to receive Jesus today, pray this simple prayer:

Father, I repent of my sin and ask You to forgive me. I open the door of my heart and invite Jesus to come in and live with me. Thank You, Lord, for saving my soul.

In Jesus Name, Amen!

After receiving Jesus I began to search for another Christian in this same church I had always attended, but people looked at me like I was crazy when I asked if they had received Jesus into their heart. I had not met anyone who declared they were a born-again believer. I was looking for someone to share this new life experience with who could teach me the Bible. Finally, I realized I had the best teacher already, the Holy Spirit!

Putting the Bible to Use

Often in those early years of being a born-again believer, the Holy Spirit would seem to make a certain Scripture sort of pop off the page at me as I read the Bible. Sometimes it seemed like the verse had neon lights on it to get my attention. I began to highlight the Scripture every time the Holy Spirit would bring it to my attention. Then each morning, before our children woke up, I would get up to pray and read my Bible. I would scan through the Bible looking for those highlighted Scriptures and pray them out loud for my family and myself.

My family and I eventually left the traditional denomination and began attending a church that was full of life and Spirit-filled believers. I loved it! I became involved in everything they had to offer! Soon after joining this church, my family also became believers and began to grow in the Lord.

While attending a church camp meeting, my husband, Dean, received Jesus just two years after I had. Our children received Jesus when I prayed with them at the ages of six and two. Later, our then four-year-old daughter went forward again to receive Jesus on her own at a Children's Crusade that was held by our church.

As the years went by, I found a wonderful Christian friend who wanted to know if I would teach her how to pray the Word. She would drive to my home in the morning after the children left for school. We would spend the time learning to pray Scriptures for our families, etc. We always prayed the Scriptures the Holy Spirit continually gave to me. I wrote them out on paper so it would be easier to pray them.

When my friend asked me if she could have a copy of *my Scripture pages*, I was not sure if I wanted to do that or not because the Holy Spirit had given them to me! But then I decided they were the Word, and the Word is for everyone. So I gave her a copy.

Throughout the years, I have added many verses to my Scripture pages. I have also given them out to many groups and distributed them to those attending my Bible studies, as well as, to everyone I counsel.

One evening at Bible study, the Lord revealed to me that there are many published books that have the Scriptures in them, but none of the books explain *how* to pray using them. So, that is what I want to help you do with this book of Scriptures and testimonies.

Before you begin to incorporate the Scriptures into your daily prayer life, I want to prepare you with some teaching about the Scriptures. They are a *tool*, not a substitute for your chat with the Lord. When you are in a difficult situation and you need an explanation or answer, find a Scripture that fits, and pray it out loud.

Why Pray a Scripture?

All Christians know that there are angels and demons! But do you realize that both are listening to the words that come out of your mouth? If they are negative words, the demons will make sure that what you speak comes to pass in your life. If the words are Scriptures, the angels will see to it that they are manifested in your life. God hastens to perform His Words, not yours! There is also power in His Word! That's why you need to pray Scripture! There is victory in God's spoken Word. Things change!

When you pray Scriptures for the first time, ask the Lord to *do* whatever the Scripture is saying.

The second time you pray them and all the rest of the times, praise Him that He *is* accomplishing it in your life. You will see things begin to happen in your life that you never thought possible.

In the Scriptures I have written, you will see the reference first and then how to speak it underneath.

Take time to look up the Scripture (the reference) for yourself so you can see the verse as it is written in the Bible. Once you do, you will have an understanding of how to incorporate praises to the Lord through other Scriptures.

For instance, when you are sick, remind God of His Word like this:

"Father, Your Word says that by Your stripes I am healed. So therefore, I praise You that I *am* healed. I command this illness, sickness, or disease to get off of me in Jesus Name. I stand in agreement with Your Word, in Jesus Name."

Now you are ready to Begin

The first thing you will want to do is take time to worship the Lord for who He is.

The following praise is a sample of what you can say:

"Father, I praise You! I praise You that You are the Rose of Sharon, the Bright and Morning Star, the Lily of the Valley, the Lion of Judah etc.", and *then add your own praise.*

After you have spent time praising Him, name the people you are praying for, yourself included, and then begin to pray the following verses out loud:

If you are praying them for yourself only, use the word, "me" or "I" instead of "us."

Praises to the Lord

Isaiah 54:17
Praise You no weapon formed against us will prosper.

Psalm 1:3
Praise You that whatever we do will prosper.

Psalm 3:3
Praise You that You are a shield for us, our glory and the lifter of our head.

Psalm 5:12
Praise You that You bless the righteous with favor and You encompass us as with a shield.

Psalm 16:11
Praise You that You are showing us the path of life and in Your Presence there is fullness of joy and at Your right hand there are pleasures forevermore.

Psalm 18:32
Praise You that You gird us with strength and make our way perfect.

Psalm 23:1
Praise You that You are our Shepherd and we shall not want.

Psalm 23:6
Praise You goodness and mercy shall follow us all the days of our lives.

Psalm 29:11
Praise You that You are our light.

Psalm 27:1
Praise You that You bless us with peace.

Psalm 31:15
Praise You that You have delivered us from persecution. I bind up all persecution from us and our families and I cast if off in Jesus' name.

Psalm 31:20
Praise You that You keep us secretly in a pavilion from the strife of tongues.

Proverbs 10:7
Praise You the memories of the just are blessed.

Psalm 32:7
Praise You that You are our hiding place and You preserve us from trouble.

Psalm 34:17
Praise You as we cry, You hear us and You deliver us out of all trouble.

Psalm 48:1
Praise You Lord, You are great and greatly to be praised.

Psalm 37:1-9
Praise You we fret not, we trust in You, we delight in You, we commit our way unto You, we rest in You, we cease from anger and we are inheriting the land. Praise You we have come into that land and we are walking in the land of prosperity and victory.

Psalm 55:22
Praise You we cast our burden upon You for You sustain (care for) us.

Any shaded boxes are great confessions to speak out loud.

Praise You that our obedience brings blessings and we receive them.

Psalm 62:6, 8
Praise You that You are our defense. We pour out our hearts before You.

Psalm 68:19
Bless You Lord, You daily load us with benefits. We receive them by faith!

Psalm 84:11
Praise You no good thing will You withhold from us who walk uprightly.

Psalm 118:24
Praise You this is the day that You have made and we are rejoicing and are glad in it.

Psalm 118:25
Praise You that You *are* sending prosperity now and we are receiving it. The demons of poverty, debt and lack are bound up and we do not receive them in our lives.

1 Thessalonians 4:12
Praise You we lack nothing.

1Timothy 6:17
Praise You that You give us richly all things to enjoy.

Psalm 119:104
Praise You through Your precepts we get understanding therefore we hate every false way.

Psalm 121:8
Praise You that You preserve our way forever.

Psalm 139:5
Praise You that You have enclosed us behind and before and Your hand is upon us.

Proverbs 2:7,8
Praise You that You are a buckler and we walk uprightly and You preserve the way of the saints.

The following box is another good confession to speak out loud.

> Praise You that all intellectualism is being brought under the captivity of the Holy Spirit and we are walking in Your love at all times.

Psalm 19:1
Praise You the words of our mouths and the meditation of our hearts are acceptable in Your sight.

Psalm 25:5
Praise You that You are leading us and teaching us and we will wait on You all the day.

Psalm 51:10, 12
Praise You that You are creating a clean heart within us and renewing a right spirit within us and restoring unto us the joy of our salvation.

Anytime you see blank lines, use them for your own verses the Lord may give you, or for notes you would like to make.

_____

_____

_____

_____

_____

_____

_____

_____

_____

_____

_____

_____

_____

_____

_____

_____

_____

Learning to be Submissive

Learning to be submissive through the Word helped me grow in the Lord. But I also began to see things in my husband that were both good and bad, so I began praying for him. I decided, now that *I* was so-o-o good, *he* needed to change too! The only problem was the more I prayed, the worse he became. One day I cried before the Lord asking Him, "Why?" Well, I sure didn't expect the answer I received. God told me He wanted *me* to change *not* my husband. What a low blow! I could hardly believe He said that to me. I thought, "Oh surely You don't mean *me*, You must be wrong." I found out, He wasn't wrong!

I began the long road of trying to be submissive to God and to my husband. That was not very easy for me, because with Dean gone away from home as much as he was; I was the whole ball game. I disciplined the children, I paid the bills, and I made all the decisions! Even when he did come home, I wore the pants in the family. I was having a hard time letting Dean make decisions.

My hunger for the Lord grew and I began talking about the Lord to some of my friends at church. I finally found a born-again believer among them! She introduced me to a Christian women's group, where I met a lot of beautiful women who were serving the Lord. It was at this time, nearly a year later, when I realized that now I had "Salvation" and understood what it meant. I was a born-again believer! A Child of God!

These Christian women were into all sorts of wonderful

Bible studies and I wanted to be in one of them too, so I offered to have one in my home. I finished one Bible study and really enjoyed it, but there was that same conviction always staring me in the face. Be submissive! Be submissive! One of the ladies mentioned a new study that was starting, on how to be a submissive wife and it only cost ten dollars and fifty cents. There was no way I could go, because we couldn't afford the ten dollars and fifty cents.

The women insisted that I *ask* my husband if I could go. I knew he would say no anyway, because we couldn't afford it. But I asked and to my surprise he said, "Yes!" He handed me the ten dollars and fifty cents right out of his pocket. I'm *still* wondering where he got that ten dollars and fifty cents from in the first place!

As I attended the class week after week, I couldn't believe I was as bad as I found out I was. I had a lot of trouble with my mouth getting into gear before I checked things out with the Lord. I had to pray the Lord would, *zip my lip* shut all the time.

Through praying Scriptures I realized I had so much to learn! My husband, of course, liked the change he saw in me and began treating me like a new bride. He bought me new clothes, brought me flowers and pampered me! The change was worth the ten dollars and fifty cents, however, I *still* haven't found out how come he had the ten dollars and fifty cents in his pocket. It must be he and the Holy Spirit were in cahoots!

If God is trying to get you or the words you speak to change, just do it. It is so much easier to allow God to have control of your life than you. You also will be blessed by your obedience to Him. Obedience always brings victory!

Hopefully, you are encouraged now to begin to pray Scripture to help you bring your mouth under control of the Holy Spirit.

Bringing your Mouth under control of the Holy Spirit

As you speak the following scriptures the Holy Spirit will help bring your mouth under control. You will begin to say things in the positive way instead of the negative.

Psalm 71:8
Our mouths are filled with praise and with Your honor all the day.

Psalm 141:13
Praise You that You are setting a watch before our mouths and keeping the door of our lips.

Another Confession

Praise You that You are helping us to serve in newness of the Holy Spirit and we are enriched in You. in all speech and all knowledge.

Ephesians 4:29
Praise You that no corrupt communication shall proceed out of our mouths but that which is good to the use of edifying, that it may minister grace unto the hearer.

Colossians 4:6
Praise You our speech is always filled with grace, seasoned with salt, so we know how to answer every man. Lord, give us words that will bless those around us.

Speak this Confession

Praise You that we speak to our families like company and our company like family.

Children

Many people are concerned about their children who are living a wrong life style. As you pray the Word of God over them, You will see the Lord change them and bring them close to Him. Entrust them to Him and know that He loves them even more than you.

Psalm 1:3
Praise You that no weapon formed against my children will prosper.

You can also plea the Blood of Jesus over them. Say: I plea the Blood of Jesus over _____ (put their name in the blank.) in Jesus Name.

You will find other Scriptures to pray for them as you learn more about praying the Word.

The following two Scriptures are great to pray not only for your children, but for your spiritual children.

Proverbs 22:6
Praise You we are training up our children (and spiritual children) in the way they should go and when they are old they will not depart from it.

Ephesians 6:1-3
Praise You our children obey us in the Lord, they are honoring their father and mother that it may be will with them and they will live long on the earth.

_____

_____

_____

_____

_____

_____

_____

_____

_____

_____

_____

Marriage

Ephesians 5:25
Praise You husbands love their own wives as Christ loved the Church and gave himself for it.

Ephesians 5:28, 33
Praise You our husbands love their own wives as they love their own bodies and themselves and *we do reverence him*.

1 Peter 4:8
Praise You husbands and wives are fervent in their love for their own spouse.

Proverbs 5:18
Praise You husbands rejoice with their own wife.

Psalm 145:16
Praise You that You satisfy the desire of every living thing. You are fulfilling our desires that are in Your perfect will.

This confession is great for your marriage.

Praise You that husbands are maturing
in the Lord, and becoming the
spiritual leaders of our homes.

More Scriptures you can pray for everyone.

Galatians 3:13
Praise You we have been redeemed from the curse of the law, for Christ became a curse for us.

Proverbs 1:23
Praise You that You are pouring out Your Holy Spirit and making known Your words to us.

Proverbs 3:4
Praise You we have found favor and good understanding in the sight of You and man.

Acts 2:21
Praise You Jerusalem is calling upon Your name and being saved.

Psalm 122:6
I pray for the peace of Jerusalem.

Romans 8:1
Praise You there is therefore no condemnation to those which are in Christ Jesus and walk according to the Holy Spirit and not the flesh.

Romans 12:2
Praise You we are not conformed to the world but we are transformed by the renewing of our minds that we may prove what is the good and acceptable and perfect will of you.

Speak this confession with authority!

> Praise You that the effect of idols in
> our lives have been bound up and
> no longer have dominion over us, or
> keep us from the proper priorities. I
> render them ineffective in our lives.

2 Corinthians 2:15
Praise You we are a sweet savor of Christ in them that are saved and in them that perish.

2 Corinthians 5:17
Praise You we are new creatures in Christ and old things are passed away, behold all things have become new.

> Praise You that the Blood of Jesus is
> over our thinking so we don't assume
> what the Holy Spirit is going to do.

Philippians 4:19
Praise You that You are supplying whatever we need according to your riches in glory.

That Scripture took on new meaning for me one year, as I began to pray it. I was amazed how God answered His Word.

The Triple Blessings

My husband had been very ill for several months. He was unable to work during that time, so our bills began to mount up. We were in great financial difficulty.

We were living in a very large house at the time which needed oil to heat and was very expensive. Our bills were all overdue! I added up everything we had, including the hospital bills from Dean's illness. It all came to about *thirty thousand* dollars! It was overwhelming to say the least.

I knew God was our Provider as He had proved Himself to us over and over in the past. So one day in prayer, I asked the Lord to give Dean ten thousand dollars in commissions for the next three months; just so we could get out of debt. I followed up that prayer with Scriptures that had to do with provision for the believer.

The first month a commission check arrived, I was excited to open it, yet I was hesitant at the same time. I ripped it open quickly, and there before my eyes, was *ten thousand dollars*! I praised God, I danced, I shouted and cried in thanksgiving all at the same time! I was never so excited to pay bills before. I kept just enough money for us to use to get us through to the next month's check.

The following month it was the same thing, another *ten thousand dollars* to pay bills. We were getting out of debt! We were so excited! Only *one* more ten thousand dollars to go and we would be able to make ends meet again. After I had prayed the various verses, I began to thank Him for His provision.

For the third month I pulled the anticipated envelope from the mailbox with his commission check in it. We needed this money! The places we owed money to were not so kind anymore and we needed to take care of the rest of the debts. I wondered if this check would be another ten thousand dollars, did the Lord answer all of my prayer, did I have the faith to believe for it?

Very slowly and with hope, I opened the envelope! Hallelujah! Praise the Lord! Thank You Lord, another *ten thousand dollars*! I thanked God so many times He must have been tired of hearing it.

Never again did we receive a commission check for ten thousand dollars. God is so faithful to His Word. I'm still overwhelmed today when I remember this awesome answer to prayer from the Lord. This was definitely a triple blessing!

I had to pray with faith and then believe that God would answer according to His Word.

I know we had been seeking the Lord on everything and I truly believed that the Bible *said if I prayed with faith*, I would receive. It looked impossible, but nothing is impossible with my God!

Miracle Provision

There was another time in our life when my husband decided to go to work for himself. He wanted to move to another city and start over with his work. I knew he could do it and I always believed that if I stood behind my husband, God would take care of us.

This would be a move of faith and trust in the Lord, believing He would provide for us.

We paid our moving expenses with Dean's *last* pay check. We were on our own and living on faith! We felt such a peace about the move. That was a miracle in itself, because we had no more income that would come in for possibly six months. As a manufacturer's representative, you first have to sell a product. Then it is made, shipped, paid for, and then you get your commission. It could take months before any income would arrive. I had figured I would get a job to tide us over, and we would be fine. The only problem was, I couldn't find a job!

We were running out of everything! The bills were going to be due soon and we didn't know what we were supposed to do. The phone rang and it was a call for Dean. He went downstairs to take the call in his new office while I went back to whatever I was doing. A little bit later he came upstairs with a big grin on his face. I thought, "Now what?"

It seems that a man we had helped financially about three years prior to this, wanted to return the favor. Only he wanted to supply Dean with a salary for six months, which would be thousands of dollars, besides that he also gave him an additional line of manufacturer's cutting tools to sell. At the end of our six months we would have to begin payments to return the money. We knew in six months we would be on our feet and doing alright, so we jumped at the chance God provided. Praise God! He is so good! Once again, God opened a door to provide for us. I never did go to work.

At the end of the six months we knew we were going to have to begin making payments to this gentleman who had helped Dean get started. It weighed on my heart because we were able to make ends meet now, but there wasn't extra to pay back anything.

This debt was in the *thousands,* not hundreds! We didn't know how we were ever going to get ahead enough to begin to pay him back.

To our surprise, that Christmas, this man and his wife sent us a card that said a simple, "Merry Christmas, debt cancelled!" We were so excited! We could hardly believe what we had just read.

As the truth of that statement began to get down into our hearts, we were filled with excitement and joy. This joy caused us to jump up and down as we praised the Lord for this awesome blessing from heaven! This was such a miracle to us that we will never forget what our wonderful Lord did as we prayed the Word. God is certainly our Provider!

A Confession for Prosperity

Praise You that the wealth of the wicked
is laid up for the just and it is coming
into our possession, pressed down,
shaken together and running over.

Philippians 4:23
Praise You the grace of Christ is with us.

Colossians 3:23
Praise You we do all things unto You and not unto men.
I give You the glory for everything in our lives.

1 Thessalonians 5:15
Praise You I do not render evil for evil unto any man.

2 Timothy 1:7
Praise You fear is not of You, for You have not given me
a spirit of fear, but a Spirit of power, of love and a sound
mind.

Colossians 3:16
Praise You the Word of Christ dwells in us (me) richly in
all wisdom and we (I) sing with grace in our (my) heart
to You.

_____

_____

_____

_____

_____

_____

_____

_____

_____

_____

Scriptures to come against the devil and his demons.

Many believers have never been taught how to fight the devil, or enemy, in their lives. Everything bad that happens is blamed on a person. Actually, a demon is able to use a person to work through to accomplish his acts. Demons want a body to use so they can function in greater measure.

In Mark 16:17 it says, "And these signs shall follow them that believe: In my name shall they cast out devils."

Jesus had authority over the demons and commanded them to go and not come back. He is our example. So, according to Mark 16:17 we know the believer has authority and power over the demons as well. The demons are forced to yield to the authority of the Name of Jesus. So as you speak in the Name of Jesus, those demons will have to obey.

That's why praying Scripture is so powerful! God hastens to perform His Word, not ours.

The following is a situation I dealt with in my life that brought me deliverance from demons.

Power in the Name of Jesus

After I had received the Baptism of the Holy Spirit and spoke in tongues, a new hunger grew within me to read. I had never enjoyed reading as much as I did now. Not only did I read more and more of my Bible, but I read all the Christian books I could get my hands on. Whenever someone would ask me if I had read a certain book and I hadn't, I would head for the Christian book store to see if there was one there. If it was and it was within my budget, I would purchase it.

One of the books that had caught my eye at the book store was called, "Out in the Name of Jesus." I skimmed through it and it looked like something I thought I needed to read. With the Holy Spirit as my teacher and guiding me into various books, I felt this was one He was prompting me to purchase. It was all about getting set free from the manifestations of evil spirits. I certainly didn't want them operating in my life, yet as I glanced at the list of them in the book, I was sure they were influencing me in a variety of ways.

After purchasing the book I hurried home to begin to read it. I had no idea of what I was about to do, or what was going to happen! My husband was working and our two children were in school so the house was all quiet and offered time for me to begin reading.

I curled myself up in the big recliner and relaxed as my excitement grew concerning this new book. I looked at the title once again and began to read! The book said, "Greater is He that is in you, than he that is in the world." 1 John 4:4

I read Mark 16:17a that said, "And these signs shall follow them that believe: In my name shall they cast out devils." And in James 4:7 it says, "Resist the devil and he will flee from you." I certainly didn't want him in my life. I wanted freedom from all these evil spirits.

I remember the book told me to be sure to forgive others before I begin to deal with demons. I needed to be sure my heart was right with the Lord. Well, as far as I knew, I was right with God.

The book talked about the things we were involved in from childhood through today such as: fortune telling, crystal balls, tea leaves, Ouija board, horoscopes, rabbit's foot, white and black magic games, involvement in secret organizations, water witching, automatic writing, charms, witchcraft, drug abuse, rock music with hidden messages and many other such things. Then the book led me in a prayer of renouncing any involvement I might have had in them.

I was so serious about this that I did whatever the book said to do. I did not want any evil spirits running my life. The Word says, "My people perish for lack of knowledge." Well, I had knowledge and I was going to get free! I was learning how much the devil is out to destroy us. He does not want us to have victory nor fulfill the plan God has for our life.

I read about the protection of the Blood of Jesus, so I spoke out loud and covered myself with the Blood of Jesus and proceeded to cast out any demons from myself. I began to name them out loud, one by one from the list in the book. I wasn't sure if I had any of them, but I wasn't going to let any stone go unturned.

Suddenly I began to cough, and cough until I was choking. Tears were coming out of my eyes and I could barely breathe. No one told me there was going to be such a showy display of these manifestations of the evil spirits.

Once I stopped all the coughing, I would continue the list in the book only to be followed by more coughing, sneezing, etc. No one told me evil spirits leave you in a variety of ways. I thought they quietly left! Little did I know! They were not happy with me, but I was not about to quit until I spoke the last word on those lists. The choking, coughing and crying finally ended and I knew the last demon was *out* in the Name of Jesus!

I sat there a few minutes trying to grasp all that had

just happened to me. I knew the Lord had taken care of me during this deliverance. So I praised Him for what He did!

As I continued to read the rest of the book, I realized I should not have done this on my own. I now needed to close the doors in my heart where I had given the demons entrance.

I also began to notice that I felt empty inside! So, I applied the Blood of Jesus to myself and then began to read the Word for a while. It was filling up that emptiness I had felt.

When I was all finished with the whole procedure and shared it with some Christian friends, we all had a big laugh at what I had done! We praised God that He was in the midst of it taking care of His child, me!

The Bible tells us that the demons will come back and check to see if the house is clean or not. If it is not, that spirit will go get seven more evil spirits, worse than what left. We are the house the Word is talking about, so that is why we need to be clean inside and continually be filled up with the Word. I had been reading the Word all along, but had not been delivered of the evil spirits yet.

I would not recommend doing this by yourself. If you want to get rid of the evil spirits in your life, have someone come and pray for you. They need to apply the Blood of Jesus over themselves as well as over you and then bind up any showy display from the evil spirits. We don't really want to give them any attention. After you do that you are ready to begin your deliverance.

You could write down the name of any evil spirits such as: anger, rejection, unforgiveness, addictions, all fears, etc. that you want to name. After you name the evil spirits, bind them up in the Name of Jesus and then command them to leave in the Name of Jesus. There is power in the Name of Jesus and the evil spirits have to obey His Name. You can learn more about the knowledge the Lord gave to me concerning deliverance and being set free in my book, "Divine Steps to Ministry."

Every time we disobey the Lord in anything. We are the ones who open the door to the enemy, so we must be quick to obey and quick to repent! God is so faithful!

My life changed after I dealt with all of that and the freedom I experienced was wonderful! Now I pray for many setting them free of evil spirits and God gives the victory!

Psalm 91:10, 11
Praise You no plague shall come near our dwelling for You have given Your angels charge over us to keep us in all our ways to bear us up in their hands lest we dash our foot against a stone.

Hebrews 1:14
Father, I ask You to commission angels to minister to us, our families, and those we pray for. Place Christians in

the path of unbelievers and those we are praying for, so they will receive as others are witnessing to them.

Psalm 59:1, 2
Praise You that You have delivered us from our enemies. You defend us from those that rise up against us and You deliver us from the workers of iniquity.

Romans 13:12
Praise You the works of darkness have been cast off from all that concerns us.

Isaiah 59:19
Praise You when the enemy comes in like a flood You lift up a standard against him.

Proverbs 6:30, 31
Praise You we have caught satan and his demons as the thief.

You are making him restore_____

(*Name what you want restored.*) For example: joy, peace, family, job, finances, possessions, love, home, etc., seven-fold of all he has robbed me of out of the substance of his house. I command him to restore it now and bring it into my possession in Jesus Name.

When you speak this out, *you* are the one in authority so you must use the word, "I" not we, or us etc.

When there is a line after a part of the Scripture, add your own words. In this case, it would be what you want him to restore, and then continue the verse. I have given you some examples.

Use the following lines to write more of what you want restored.

_____

_____

_____

_____

_____

_____

_____

_____

_____

Matthew 18:18
Praise You whatsoever I bind on earth is bound in heaven. Therefore, I bind up the demons from influencing our friends, families, those we work with, or our neighbors.

Remember, demons use people to accomplish the negative things in your life. So, stop looking at the individual people and know it's the demons using them. They most likely aren't even aware of it.

Isaiah 54:14
Praise You we are far from oppression, torment and terrorism. We will not fear, for it will not come near us. We bind up oppression, torment and terrorism and command it to leave now, in Jesus Name.

It's very important for you to put this armor on every day!

God's armor protects you on every side but the back. That's because you need to face the enemy and fight with the Word, knowing God has your back.

Ephesians 6:11-12, 14-18
Praise You we have on Your whole armor. We gird up our loins with truth. We have on the breastplate of righteousness. Our feet are shod with the preparation of the Gospel of peace. We take the shield of faith wherewith we are able to quench all the fiery darts of the wicked and we have on the helmet of Salvation. We have the sword of the Spirit which is the Word of God and we pray always with all prayer and supplication in the Spirit, watching thereunto with all perseverance and supplication for all saints.

Ephesians 5:11
Praise You we have no fellowship with the unfruitful works of darkness, but rather we reprove them in Jesus Name.

Galatians 5:1
Praise You we stand fast in the liberty where Christ *has* set us free and we are not entangled in the yolk of bondage.

Romans 8:15, 17
Praise you we have *not* received the spirit of bondage again to fear, but we *have* received the Spirit of adoption, whereby we cry, Abba, Father, for we *are* the children of God and joint heirs with Christ.

2 Corinthians 10:4
Praise You Lord the weapons of our warfare are not carnal but are mighty through you to the pulling down of strongholds. I therefore pull down all the strongholds of the enemy and bind them up in Jesus Name. I cast them off and render the mission of the enemy canceled in Jesus Name.

Colossians 1:13, 14
Praise You that You have delivered us from the power of darkness and translated us into the kingdom of Your Son in whom we have redemption, even the forgiveness of sins.

_____

_____

_____

_____

_____

_____

_____

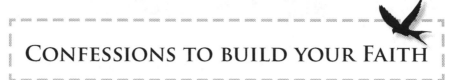

CONFESSIONS TO BUILD YOUR FAITH

Romans 5:19
Praise You by our obedience many are being made righteous.

Romans 8:5
Praise You we live in accordance with You, Holy Spirit, and we have our minds set on what the Holy Spirit desires. Lord, keep our minds on You so we remain single-minded.

Exodus 23:20
Praise You that You send angels before us to keep us on the way and You are bringing us into the place which You have prepared.

Exodus 23:25
We serve You Lord and You bless our bread and our water and take away sickness from the midst of us and the number of our days You will fulfill.

Praise You that You bless and sanctify everything that goes into our mouths today.

Matthew 5:16
Praise You our lights shine before men. They are seeing our good works and are glorifying You Father, which are in heaven.

Philippians 1:27
Praise You my family and I are standing fast in one spirit with one mind, striving together for the faith of the Gospel. We are like-minded and we have the same love. We are of one accord, of one mind and nothing is being done through strife or vain glory.

Jeremiah 42:3
Praise You that You are showing us the way where we may walk and the things that we may do.

Jeremiah 20:11
Praise You that You are with us as a mighty terrible one, therefore our persecutors shall stumble and they shall not prevail, they shall be greatly ashamed.

Luke 10:19
Praise You that You have given unto us power to tread on serpents and demonic powers and over all the power of the enemy and nothing shall by any means hurt us.

Psalm 119:18
Praise You that You are opening our eyes and we are beholding wonderful things from Your Word. Praise You the eyes of our understanding are open.

Psalm 119:125
Praise You that You have made us Your servants, and we have understanding.

Philippians 1:27
Praise You we conduct ourselves in a manner worthy of the Gospel at all times and in all places.

2 Thessalonians 3:2
Praise You we have been delivered from perverse and evil men.

1 John 2:16
Praise You that You are keeping us from the lust of the flesh, lust of the eyes, and the pride of life. I bind them up from influencing us in Jesus Name.

1 John 3:22
Praise You whatsoever we ask, we receive of You because we are keeping Your commandments and doing those things that are pleasing in Your sight.

Romans 8:11
Praise You Your Word has quickened us.

A Good Confession Wins
Knees Bite the Pavement

It was a beautiful day in the summer of 1999 and my daughter and I were going shopping. She and her husband were expecting their first baby. My husband and I were very excited because we would have a little grandchild living right near us. Our other grandchildren lived in Florida with our son and his wife and we did not get to see them very often. After all, grandparents are supposed to be able to spoil the grandchildren and we wanted to do lots of that.

My daughter and I headed out the door towards the car. I had my arms full and went around the front of the car to get in on the passenger side. As I turned towards the door, the heel of my shoe caught in the crack of the cement, causing me to lose my balance and fall. As my knees jabbed onto the cement, I felt extreme pain, to say the least. Within seconds I could feel blood running down the shin of my legs, especially the right one.

I was not sure how I was going to get up because the pain was so severe. My daughter was in no condition to even *try* to lift or help me. I sat on the pavement trying to figure out how to get to the door of the car so I could lean on it and pull myself up. I couldn't bear any weight on the knees like you would normally in order to get up. I was stuck! We prayed and the idea came to me for her to get a pillow from the house to put under my knees. I thought maybe I could use it to get something soft under my knee, so I could lean on it and then I could get up into the car.

She brought out a bed pillow that was soft and slid it under my knee as I raised myself up a little. It seemed like a long slow process, but finally I was able to lift myself onto the seat of the car. I sat there a minute rocking back and forth in pain, still feeling the blood running down my leg. My pants had a large wet spot on the knee from the blood, but the other one didn't seem to be bleeding.

We sat there in the driveway for a few minutes while I tried to recover. She thought we should cancel the shopping trip, but I didn't want to. I told her just to drive and that by the time we get to the store on the other side of town, *I would be fine*. I laid my hand on my knees and prayed as I quoted Scriptures. My daughter agreed with me. The Word says in Matthew 18:19, "Where two or more agree as touching anything it shall be done for them of my Father which is in Heaven."

When we arrived at the store, I wasn't sure if I would be able to walk. I also thought if there was blood all over my pants, they would not look very nice. I looked down at my pants as my daughter opened my car door. I could hardly believe my eyes. There was *nothing* on my knee at all! The pants were *dry*, and the blood was *gone*! Wow!

I tried to pull the pants up my leg a bit to see, but the pants were too tapered to accomplish the task. I put my pant leg down and decided to take a step. Actually, I still did not know if I could stand or walk. I stepped out onto the ground by the car and slowly stood. The pain wasn't so bad, it was the bending of the knees that hurt when I walked. The movement of the joint did not feel very good either.

We walked into the store and I moved rather slowly, but with each step it seemed a bit better. I could still feel the blood running down the front of my shin, but couldn't *see* it.

I was so uncomfortable we did not shop for long. When we got back to my house I went to check my knees and clean up the blood, but to my surprise, there was *nothing* to clean up! No blood, no skinned knee, nothing! I did not even have a bruise! I could hardly believe my eyes!

I did have some pain and soreness for a long time, but eventually even that went away. God is so good to bring us healing!

I believe the confession I spoke out of my mouth, "By the time we get to the other side of town I would be fine", brought healing even before we spoke the Scriptures. God is our Healer yesterday, today, and forever! He is always the same!

Psalm 119:89
Praise You Your Word is forever settled in heaven.

2 Timothy 2:9
Praise You Your Word is not bound.

Jeremiah 1:12
Praise You that You hasten to perform Your Word.

2 Chronicles 6:10
Praise You that You have performed Your Word.

Psalm 103:20
Bless You Lord, Your angels mighty in strength perform Your Word.

Hebrews 4:12
Praise You Your word is quick and powerful and sharper than any two-edged sword.

Psalm 138:2
Praise You that You magnify Your Word above Your name.

Deuteronomy 8:3
Praise You we live by Your Word.

Philippians 4:13
Praise You we can do all things through Christ.

Matthew 17:20
Praise You nothing is impossible with You.

A Death Sentence

One year I was invited to be a special speaker at a church for a women's Bible study. I was excited for the opportunity to share.

After prayer and preparation, I was on my way. The meeting was held in the Sanctuary first for some praise and worship and then we went into a much smaller room where I spoke.

After the session, several ladies shared how much they enjoyed what I had shared. One lady apologized to me that she wouldn't be able to come next week because she was going to have heart surgery. She said the doctors didn't expect her to make it through the surgery. It was a death sentence for sure!

My heart was so touched by this sweet lady who sat there with tears welling up in her eyes. I asked her if I could pray for her not knowing if she even believed in *divine* healing. She said she would like that, so I prayed a simple prayer for her. I laid my hand high up on her chest by her neck and asked the Lord to give her a new heart! I had *never* prayed for anyone to receive a new heart before. She thanked me and we said good bye.

After everyone had left, the pastor's wife informed me that the lady had been sick quite a long time with a bad heart and this surgery was her last chance at life. I couldn't get the lady off my mind. To know you were headed for surgery and might not make it through must have been a hard thing for her to face.

I prayed for her a little during the week and then went about my business. I didn't even know what day her surgery was to be.

The following week I went back for one more special meeting at the ladies Bible study. We had the time of praise and worship and then headed into the smaller room, like we had before. As we entered the room, I was surprised to see that *same lady* sitting in there waiting for us. I went right to her to greet her. I asked her how come she was there. I know it was a dumb question, but I thought she might be in the hospital recovering. I *did* expect her to recover from the surgery!

She grabbed my hand and said she had a doctor's visit the day before her surgery and they couldn't find one thing wrong with her heart!

God had given her a new heart!

Why is it, that when we pray with faith and believing, and God answers what we prayed for, we are surprised? That was the first of many other times the Lord used me to bring healing to others. Hearts seemed to be on the top of His list at the time.

I had lots of growing to do to minister healing, and He has been faithful to His *Word* to bring it to pass! Thank You Lord!

More New Body Parts

The Lord has used me to bring healing to people on many occasions. But several that come to my thinking are the ones where He has given them a *new organ*.

One lady in my church was having trouble with her lungs. One day she asked me to lay hands on her and pray. I saw *new lungs* go into her by the Spirit and she received them. She is well to this day.

A man in the church who had a bad liver was also given a death sentence. As he began to grow in the Lord and change his life style, he had the faith to believe for a *new liver*. He asked me to pray for him, so I did. God did give him a new liver! Now he is serving the Lord in health.

Another time a lady in church, who had lots of intestinal problems for most of her life, came forward for prayer. As I laid my hands on her and began to pray, I noticed something moving in my peripheral spiritual vision. I saw a long rope that was twisted and coming toward us from the ceiling. Suddenly, it began to go inside of her and swirl around and around. God had just given her a *new intestine*. She reported back that she had no trouble in her body for the first time in years. God is in the business of healing and giving new parts, but each person has to receive.

God has much for us in the future but our part is to pray, believe and *receive*!

James 5:16
Praise You the effective prayer of a righteous man can accomplish much and today we are accomplishing much through our prayers.

2 Corinthians 13:14
Praise God the grace of Jesus, the love of God and the fellowship of the Holy Spirit is with us all.

Maybe as you continue to read your Bible you will come across verses that will affirm your faith. As you do, jot them down on the lines below and then add them to your prayer time.

Remember to always speak the Scriptures out loud. Just thinking them does not accomplish anything. You need to hear them so the truth goes down into your spirit. Then when a situation arises, you have the verses within you which the Holy Spirit is able to draw from. He will be able to bring the Scripture to your remembrance, in the midst of a situation when you don't have the book.

_____

_____

_____

_____

_____

_____

_____

HEALING

Matthew 6:10
Thy Kingdom come. Thy will be done in earth, as it is in heaven.

There is no sickness in heaven, so we know it's God's will for us to be healed on earth.

The following Scriptures are affirmations, written as praises to help encourage you as you believe God for your total healing.

3 John 1:2
Praise You we are prospering and *are* in health as our soul prospers.

1 Peter 2:24
Praise You by Your stripes we *are* already healed.

Proverbs 4:21,22
Praise You Your Word does not depart from before our eyes, for Your Word is life unto us and health to our *flesh*.

Isaiah 53:5
Praise You, Jesus was wounded for my transgressions and bruised for my sin. The chastisement for my peace was put on Him on the cross and by His stripes I *am* healed.

Psalm 103: 3-5

Praise You that You have healed all our diseases, You have redeemed our lives from destruction, crowned us with lovingkindness, tender mercies and satisfied our mouth with good things, so that our youth is renewed like the eagle's.

We know God is Sovereign and He can do anything! We know He can heal us in a variety of ways. I prefer to stand in faith and not undergo surgery. But sometimes we have to stop standing and waiting because we can get into presumption that God is going to *always* heal us supernaturally.

The devil wants us to get into presumption until we die just because we decided to stand in faith. Well, it takes faith to go through surgery too. It is always up to the Lord as to the direction you are to go.

He has healed me many times miraculously, so I was surprised when I had to go through surgery one particular time.

Being a Spirit-filled believer, I had spent time praying over every detail of the coming surgery. I prayed over the instruments, nurses, doctors, operating equipment and the operating room. I also prayed I would have no pain. Everything was covered in prayer that I could think of. I even prayed that I wouldn't have to have any transfusions.

I had surgery in the afternoon and was told it was one

of the worst surgeries this doctor had ever had to perform. He called in two other doctors to help him. He said there was a growth with feelers attached that went throughout my body and wrapped themselves around my organs. He had to move the organs and scrape the residue off. I was told I didn't even bleed! I of course was totally unaware of this when I woke up that evening.

I didn't feel too badly, I was just tired of course. The nurses kept coming into my room to give me shots for pain, but I didn't want them. They insisted on it for a while until I said, "I don't need the shot, *I don't have any pain!*" God was answering my prayers.

There was an elderly lady in the bed next to mine. She had surgery a couple of days before I did. But about two in the morning she was crying and crying and didn't seem to get any help.

The nurses were on strike so there wasn't much help on the floor for the patients. I kept ringing the buzzer for her because she couldn't reach hers. Finally, I asked her if there was something I could do for her. She was desperate for a drink of water, and also needed something for pain. I finally decided *I had to help* her!

I hadn't been out of bed yet myself since my surgery, and was a little concerned if I *could* get up by myself or not. I decided I would trust the Lord to help me and give me strength as well as His grace to help her.

I slowly got up and sat on the edge of my bed a minute; that in itself was a task. Finally, I stood up and started to shuffle along to her far side of the bed as I held onto the bed and my stomach. It seemed like I was walking a mile, because every little inch I stepped, it hurt. I got over to the other side of her bed and helped her take a drink of water.

Suddenly, the Holy Spirit quickened in my heart to lay my hands on her and pray for her to have a peaceful sleep. I asked her if I could pray for her and she said I could. I laid my hands on her and prayed. She had been crying for hours, literally hours, whimpering and whimpering in pain.

As soon as I had finished praying for her I shuffled back to my own bed, more than ready to lie down and get off of my feet. Before I was even back in bed, she had fallen asleep. She never did get her medication, but she did have a peaceful night's sleep after we prayed. Thanks to the Lord!

There is much more to this story but you will have to read about it in my book, "Healing and the Miraculous."

Mark 16:17-18
And these signs shall follow them that believe; In My Name shall they cast out devils; they shall speak with new tongues; they shall take up serpents; and if they drink any deadly thing, it shall not hurt them; they shall lay hands on the sick, and *they shall recover.*

Psalm 118:17
Praise You we shall not die, we shall live and declare the works of the Lord.

Jeremiah 30:17
Praise You that You restore health to my body and healing to all my wounds.

Psalm 91
Praise You that You have set Your love upon me and deliver me. You have set me on high because I know Your Holy Name. I call on You and You answer me. You are with me in times of trouble. You deliver and honor me and satisfy me with *long life* as You continually show me Your Salvation.

Proverbs 16:24
Praise You our words are as pleasant as honeycomb, sweet to the soul and healing to the bones.

Psalm 103:3
Praise You for forgiving me of all my iniquities and You have healed all my diseases.

Psalm 107:20
Praise You that You sent Your Word and healed me. You have delivered me from my own destruction.

Psalm 41:3
Praise You Lord for strengthening me in times of illness. You have sustained Me.

Proverbs 4:20-22
Praise You for helping me obey when You call me Your child and ask me to pay attention to Your Words and listen to what You have to say. I do not let Your Word depart from my eyes. I keep Your Word in my heart because I know that it is life to my spirit and health to my flesh.

Matthew 9:35
Praise You Jesus for healing every sickness and every disease among the people.

Matthew 10:1
…He gave them power against unclean spirits, to cast them out, and to heal all manner of sickness and all manner of disease.

Hebrews 13:8
Praise You Jesus is the same yesterday, today and forever. *He heals me today just like He healed in Bible times.*

Mark 7:37
He has done all things well: He makes both the deaf to hear, and the dumb to speak.

James 5:14-16
God's Word says I am to call for the elders of the church and let them pray over me and anoint my body with oil in the Name of the Lord. And the prayer of faith shall save the sick, and the Lord shall raise him up; and if he has committed sins, they shall be forgiven. Confess your

faults one to another, and pray one for another, that you may be healed.

Matthew 4:23
Praise You that Jesus went about and healed all manner of sickness and all manner of disease; *and He has healed me.*

A Confession for Healing

Praise You Lord, that Jesus took all our sicknesses and diseases to the cross so we wouldn't have to have it. I choose to believe He did it for me, and my body is already healed.

Sickness is leaving my body.

Disease (dis-ease) is leaving my body.

I am healed in Jesus Name!

Jesus loves you so much He died for you. Speak these Scriptures and confessions out loud daily. The words will go back into your own ears and down into your heart. As that happens, your body will begin to conform to what you speak. It may not conform overnight, but it will happen if you pray with faith and believing. Don't quit! Pray until you get the desired result. It is God's good pleasure to answer your prayers!

HE LOVES YOU!

PRAYER OF SALVATION

Meet my best friend, Jesus! If you don't know Jesus as your personal Lord and Savior and want to have the best friend you will ever have, pray this prayer:

Father,

I believe Jesus is the Son of God. I believe Jesus died on the cross for my sins and that He rose from the dead. I ask You to forgive me for all the things I have said, thought, or done wrong. I am sorry! I open the door of my heart and invite You, Jesus, to come in and live with me. Be the Lord of my life. I also ask You to fill me up to overflowing with Your Holy Spirit.

I believe I am now saved, *born-again,* and I am a child of God. I believe I have eternal life.

Thank You, Lord, for saving my soul! Amen!

Sign your name here so you remember the special day you received Jesus.

_____

Sign your name here

Today's date is _____.

If you have prayed the prayer of Salvation for the first time, I would like to send you a free booklet entitled "Set Free." Please send me your name and address in an email to receive the booklet.

revjoanhart@hart2heart.net

Author's Note

You will notice a small "s" is used for satan's name. This is because in my estimation he is not worth the capitalization of his name.

You will also notice certain words that are not usually capitalized according to the standard grammatical practice. This has been done in this book for the purpose of respect for the Lord and His Word.

BOOKS BY JOAN HART

How to Have Victory through Prayer

You might go through life needing answers to your problems, needs and hurts, or desires and not realize prayer can destroy any force the devil might use against you. In this book you will find the answers you have searched for and how to apply them to your life, as well as, how Joan found Jesus and received Him as her Savior.

How to Have Victory through Prayer CD

Audio CD of the Scriptures used in the book, How To Have Victory Through Prayer. They will allow you to pray them as you drive, or while you are getting ready for the day. The Scriptures will get down into your heart and then when you need a verse that fits your situation, the Holy Spirit will be able to bring it to your remembrance so you can pray it, bringing you victory!

Phenomena of the Holy Spirit

When Jesus took Joan to the Throne Room or into Heaven for a visit it changed her life forever.

Each chapter written is an individual story about the awesome power of the Holy Spirit as He was revealed in a variety of ways in Joan's life. Through her intimacy with the Lord, Joan has had many phenomenal experiences.

Faith and the Supernatural

When Jesus took Joan through many trials of her faith, it caused her to grow spiritually and taught her how to trust the Lord no matter what happened.

She was also allowed the privilege of a chariot ride to Heaven which changed her life forever. These stories are about some of those encounters.

Healing and the Miraculous

It has been more than forty years since God miraculously healed Joan. Read and find out how she was miraculously set free from excruciating pain of the physical disorders she dealt with.

God in His mercy, power and love, totally healed her forever, as well as prepared her for a prophetic ministry.

Divine Steps to Ministry

The Lord led Joan through each Divine step toward the ministry she has today.

Some of the stories are serious while others are quite funny, yet all of them took Joan on a path toward greater obedience in serving the Lord.

Be encouraged and filled with new hope as you become aware of God's Divine steps in your own life.

CONTACT

To order books or to find out more information about Joan's ministry, write or call:

Hart to Heart Ministries
Christian Training Center

Books from the Hart
7281 Sandpiper Street,
Portage, MI 49024
269-388-8075

E-mail: revjoanhart@hart2heart.net

Web: www.hart2heart.nct

Printed in the United States
By Bookmasters